dumbthings
shedoes

dumbthings shedoes

holly wagner

© 1999 by Holly Wagner. All rights reserved

Printed in the United States of America

Packaged by WinePress Publishing, PO Box 1406, Mukilteo, WA 98275. The views expressed or implied in this work do not necessarily reflect those of WinePress Publishing. Ultimate design, content, and editorial accuracy of this work are the responsibilities of the author(s).

No part of this publication may be reproduced, stored in a retrieval system, or transmitted in any way by any means—electronic, mechanical, photocopy, recording, or otherwise—without the prior permission of the copyright holder except as provided by USA copyright law.

Unless otherwise noted all scriptures are taken from the New King James Version, Copyright © 1979, 1980, 1982 by Thomas Nelson, Inc., Publishers. Used by permission.

ISBN 1-57921-203-4
Library of Congress Catalog Card Number: 98-83200

Dedication

This book is dedicated
to those of you reading this;
to those committed to building
a strong marriage in a society
that so desperately needs
to see you succeed.
You *can* do it!

Thanks . . .

. . . to my Father in heaven for such an awesome call and awesome life; I am so grateful to be alive on the planet at this time in history!

. . . to Philip, who has loved me and continues to love me in spite of all the dumb things I do!!

. . . to Jordan and Paris, two of the greatest children, and who continue to make life exciting!

. . . to the people of the Oasis Christian Center, who have given me the opportunity to grow and pursue God's purpose.

. . . to Noriko for all of the typing and computer help.

. . . to Shanelle, Lisa, Dad, and Bu for the never-ending encouragement.

. . . to Marilyn, Bunny, Betty, Wendy, Bobbie, and Chris for the kind words.

Contents

Preface xi
Introduction xiii

DUMB THINGS SHE DOES

CHAPTER ONE: Not Liking Yourself—
What's Not to Like? 19
CHAPTER TWO: Not Demonstrating Respect to Him—
R-E-S-P-E-C-T, Just Like the Song Says! 29
CHAPTER THREE: Trying to Fix Him—
Not That He Doesn't Need a Good Fixing! 39
CHAPTER FOUR: Not Getting Involved in What He's Doing—
He Really Does Want You There 49

CHAPTER FIVE: Being a Dream Stealer—
C'mon, Cheer Him on Girls! 53
CHAPTER SIX: Not Understanding Your Role—
Take a Deep Breath before Reading This One! 57

DUMB THINGS WE BOTH DO

CHAPTER ONE: Not Forgiving—
Go Ahead, Say "I'm Sorry" 67
CHAPTER TWO: Not Fighting Fair—
Yes, There Are Rules! 75
CHAPTER THREE: Not Understanding Our Differences—
Viva la Difference! 79
CHAPTER FOUR: Expect a Great Marriage to Just Happen—
Cinderella Was a Fairy Tale! 87
CHAPTER FIVE: One Last Thing—
And I Do Mean That! 93

Preface

"Remind me that God hates divorce and that murder is against the law!" was a plea I made to a good friend a few years ago. I laugh about that comment now, but back then I wasn't kidding. Not only did it seem that our marriage just wasn't fun anymore, but maintaining it was too much work. Perhaps there have been times when you, too, have felt like that. Perhaps you are feeling like that now! Well, take heart; you are not alone, and there are some answers!

In this book I will present some clear, simple suggestions that certainly helped my marriage and that I believe will help yours. This book is not the ultimate guide to wedded bliss; it does not present all the answers to every problem. This book is just a small piece of the puzzle. There are many books on marriage out there; read some. There are wonderful seminars and conferences available to help us married people; go to one. A great marriage doesn't happen just because you want it, but because you want it enough to learn and grow.

I split this book into three sections, "Dumb Things She Does," "Dumb Things We Both Do," and "Dumb Things He Does." Read whatever section applies to your situation, or read them all. And after reading, *talk*. Talk to your spouse about what you've read. Do you agree with this point or that point? Have you done this particular dumb thing? (Let your spouse answer as to whether you have done one of the dumb things or not!) Remember marriages are worked out over a lifetime, so relax. . . . Even you—no matter how many dumb things you've done—*can* strengthen your marriage!

Introduction

Marriages, both Christian and non-Christian, are crumbling at an alarming rate all over our country and the world. Rarely does a marriage fall apart because some outside force has attacked. Even in the case when one spouse leaves the other for another man or woman, that is usually the result of damage that has been done in the marriage months or years earlier. Just as it takes years for a marriage to grow strong and solid, it also takes time for a marriage to fall apart.

It is our job as spouses to protect our marriage and to make as many good choices as possible! In Mark 10:7–9 Jesus says,

> For this reason a man shall leave his father and mother and be joined to his wife, and the two shall become one flesh; so then they are no longer two, but one flesh. Therefore what God has joined together, let not man separate.

God is telling us not to separate and not to destroy what He has brought together. The process of two becoming one is not always an easy one. In fact, it can be quite messy!

So many times in counseling sessions, one spouse will complain that he or she just doesn't love the other spouse anymore. I would like to suggest that love is not just a feeling: it is not just a place we fall into, it is not just something we're in—it is something that we *do*, regardless of how we feel. Feelings come and go. We can't base our marriages on feelings.

I was raised watching *Cinderella,* which in itself isn't bad, but I actually believed in the Prince-Charming, happily-ever-after stuff. Imagine my surprise when Philip, my husband, didn't always act like Prince Charming. "Happily ever after" came only after serious work and communication and the laying down of my ego. No, that was definitely not mentioned in the fairytale.

One of my favorite movies is *Sleepless in Seattle*, and after seeing it, one of my girlfriends remarked that a part-two would be great. I quickly commented that I wasn't too sure it would be an appealing movie because part-two would just be the couple working out their relationship like the rest of us!

Our job is to keep from destroying what He's brought together and to continue the difficult process of two becoming one. Because it's His plan, with His help we can do it.

So let's get ready to look at some of the dumb things we've all done, and what we can do to bring change. Let's strengthen our marriages so that, not only are our homes happier places to be, but also we truly will be a light in a dark world.

Dumb Things She Does . . .

Chapter One

NOT LIKING YOURSELF—
WHAT'S NOT TO LIKE?

It is not your husband's job to give you a life. It is not his job to make you feel good about yourself. While he wants to be your hero, it is not his job to fix you. In Mark 12:31 Jesus tells us to love our neighbor as ourselves. He is telling me that I won't be effective at loving anyone else if I don't love myself—if I don't love who God made me to be. Philip is not responsible for my self-esteem. I am. It is up to me to know that God loves me and has a purpose for me.

When you like who you are, it makes you more fun to be around. You laugh at mistakes, not taking yourself and

DUMB THINGS SHE DOES . . .

everything around you so seriously. You're comfortable with yourself. One evening a few years ago, Philip was speaking at another church in our city. I was there with him to be supportive and to talk to the congregation about his books and tapes that were being sold in the back of the room. I was addressing the congregation and explaining what was on some of his tapes. It was my first time doing this, and after describing a few tapes, I decided to give some away. I then thought that rather than handing the tape to someone, I would throw it to her. Obviously I need to work on my throwing arm, because instead of the tape reaching the woman I had intended it for, the tape beaned some poor, unsuspecting man in the head.

I felt terrible! My first time on the job, and I blew it! The poor man, with his eye watering, was trying to be brave as I handed him a tissue, cracked a few jokes on myself, and carried on. (I think my husband slid under his chair at this point!) Now, did I make a mistake? Yes. Have I since learned some cassette-tape distribution etiquette? Yes. Did it rob me of my confidence? No. When you make mistakes and goof up, be willing to laugh. I'm not talking about serious, life-threatening mistakes. Those aren't funny. But sometimes our inability to laugh at ourselves is a sure sign that we lack confidence or self-esteem. We need to learn to like who we are—warts and all!

Not Liking Yourself

There are a lot of reasons for low self-esteem. Past abuse, neglect, rejection, and abandonment are just a few confidence-stealers. All of us at one point or another have experienced some of these; some of us have experienced devastating abuse. Regardless, the important thing is to begin a plan to build self-esteem. The self-esteem, I am talking about is *not* the self-centered, as-long-as-I'm-happy-it's-OK mentality, nor is it arrogance. I'm talking about the quiet confidence you get from knowing your identity, from knowing that God put you on the planet for a purpose. There are certainly men who need to understand this, but in my limited experience, I have seen more women struggle with the issue of self-esteem.

In many states, the legal drinking age is twenty-one, so to get into some facilities where alcohol is served, you must show an ID, proving that you are at least twenty-one. Many teens, wanting to get into the clubs, borrow someone else's ID to get in. Some of us today are using borrowed IDs, not only to get into God's kingdom, but also to get through life. We can't do this! I have to know who I am in God. I have to know who He's made me to be. As much as I love my husband, I won't get into heaven on his coattails, nor will I fulfill my purpose on the earth until I become the woman God created me to be. So I need to know who that woman is!

One of the reasons we must know who we are, is to determine what we'll do. We can't do this backward. I can't rely on what I do to determine who I am, because if what I do is snatched away or if I fail at it, then I'll see myself as a loser. Michelle Kwan is a phenomenal ice skater, but what happens when she can no longer skate? She will struggle if her only identity is in being a skater. What about the Tiger Woodses, Michael Jordans, and beauty queens of the world? What happens when they can no longer do what they now do? Will they lose personal confidence? Will they be confused or depressed? What about you? Is your identity wrapped up in what you do?

God gives us an identity before He gives us a job to do. In the Old Testament we read that before Abram became the father of many nations, he was given a new identity. God changed his name from Abram to Abraham, which means "father of many nations" (see Gen. 17). In the Book of Judges, God gave Gideon a new identity. Gideon saw himself as the least in his family and saw his family as being the weakest in the whole town (Judg. 6:15). Before God asked Gideon to build an army and defeat the Midianites, He called him a mighty man of valor. God gave Gideon a new identity.

As believers and followers of Christ, you and I have been given a new identity. We don't get our identity from our driver's

Not Liking Yourself

license; most of the stuff on that is embellished anyway! We don't get our identity from our passport; that just tells us where we've been. We don't get our identity from school report-cards; most of us are still dealing with the negative things some teachers said. We don't get our identity from a mirror; we just use that to put on makeup. You and I get our identity from our creator. God tells us who we are. It's through His eyes and His Word, that we get a true picture of who we are. God says that we are:

- Not victims, but conquerors—in fact, more than conquerors (Rom. 8:37)
- Not our parent's "accident," but known by God from the womb, and destined with a purpose (Jer. 1:4–5)
- Not a loser, but a winner (2 Chron. 2:14)
- Not an addict, but an overcomer (Luke 4:18–19)
- Not sickly, but healed (Isa. 53:5)
- Not a captive, but set free (Luke 4:18–19)
- Not a sinner, but forgiven (Eph. 4:32)
- Not poor, but rich (Prov. 10:22)
- Not a random creation, but put on the earth "for such a time as this." (Esther 4:14)

As Christians we have been given a new identity. Our self-esteem should come from knowing who we are in Christ, knowing that we are special to God. God calls us His chosen generation, a royal priesthood, and a holy nation. We are His called-with-a-purpose, special people! (1 Pet. 2:9).

You can't get self-esteem from reading books, although they're often helpful. You can't get it from going to seminars, although you'll learn a lot! Self-esteem comes, first of all, from living in the identity God has given you, regardless of the circumstances. Secondly, self-esteem comes from daring to dream, following through on the dream, and suffering through all the sacrifice and pain necessary to reach the dream. Then, when you finally reach the goal, the dream, you are so impressed with yourself that your self-esteem and your self-confidence rises.

One of my weaknesses was not finishing projects once I started them. I am a great starter! It's just my finishing that needs work! Because I saw myself as weak in this area, it affected my self-confidence. I knew I needed a plan. I knew I needed to start something and then actually finish it. At this time, I was taking my son, Jordan, to karate class. As I watched the classes, I began to think, *I can do this.* Plus, I noticed that at every level a student passed, a new color of belt was given, all the way to the black belt. It was like a prize, and I like prizes!

So, I signed up for karate. Perhaps this wasn't the easiest of goals for me to reach, but this is what I did. I started as a white

Not Liking Yourself

belt, and at every class I attended, I looked at the black-belt on the wall and said, *You're mine!* Four years later, I passed my black-belt test. Was it hard? Yes! Were there times I wanted to quit? Yes! Were there times it was inconvenient? Yes! Just the fact that this was a difficult goal to finish, made it even more valuable to me. Getting my black belt did things for my self-esteem that nothing else had done up to that point. I had started something and finished it! You can too. Pick something, anything. Find a goal, and begin the process of reaching it. When you do, you will feel amazing!

When a woman is confident in who God made her to be, she has a healthy self-esteem, and there is no occasion for envy. Think about it. Why would you be envious of someone else? Because you want what they have, and you don't trust that God loves you enough to take care of you. I am always amazed at people who can really sing. I mean, there are women who can actually stay on key for an entire song! It baffles my mind! Because I can't sing a note (or at least not the right note), I could be envious and look at a woman who can sing, wanting what she has. But I would be wasting my valuable time, wanting a gift God has given to someone else, instead of being thankful for the abilities He's given me. None of us was created with the exact same purpose, same personality, or same destiny. We are each unique and have a specific plan from God. We each need to spend time discovering what our purpose is, instead of wanting some one else's. That only leads to frustration and envy. Come on, sisters, let's rejoice when one of us accomplishes something, is honored for a talent she has, or gets married. Don't be envious and wonder why it didn't happen to you. Remember who God says you are! He created you to be special and to fulfill a unique purpose. Find out what it is.

In the Book of Proverbs, chapter 31, a question is asked: Who can find a virtuous wife? *Virtuous*, in this context, doesn't mean "quiet, weak, or able to crochet," which is what I always thought (which is also why being virtuous seemed boring to me!). In my study, however, I discovered that a virtuous woman involves three different qualities bound together. First, she has strength. She is a person with might and valor. She is not a weakling! Secondly, *virtuous* actually means "to be a member of an army." So, she is a force on the earth. Look around you; you are part of an army of women who are walking the journey with you. Thirdly, the virtuous woman has riches, substance, wealth, and knows what to do with it. This woman—you—is amazing. And she was amazing *before* the man in Proverbs ever came along. He is looking for a virtuous woman.

Not Liking Yourself

I am not to wait for a man, my husband, to make me virtuous. No, that responsibility is in my lap. Marriage should be a place where two wholes meet, not a place to get neediness met.

> **Make a plan to build your confidence in who God says you are. You can do it!**

Chapter Two

NOT DEMONSTRATING RESPECT TO HIM—
R-E-S-P-E-C-T, JUST LIKE THE SONG SAYS!

... let the wife see that she respects her husband.
—Ephesians 5:33*b*

YOUR HUSBAND'S NUMBER-ONE NEED is to feel respected. Actually, God is asking us to demonstrate respect to our husband, whether he "deserves" it or not. If there are occasions when you are having a hard time respecting what he does, then respect his position as head of your home. I don't always respect the decisions the president of our country makes, but I always respect the position of presidency. Likewise, God asks the husband to demonstrate love to us at all times, even when we are unlovable. (Yes, it's hard to believe, but sometimes we are hard to love!) God is asking both of us to submit to His leadership by laying down our egos and our rights and, instead, preferring the other. We both have a tough job, because I know there are times when I am not very loveable, but that doesn't change what my husband is asked to do. And there are times when it takes a conscious decision of my will to demonstrate respect to my husband when what I want to do is very loudly give him several pieces of my mind! Nevertheless, my job, because I am submitted to God's plan for my life, is to demonstrate respect to my husband.

There are a few ways we can show respect. The first way is in how we talk *about* him:

> Her husband is known in the gates when he sits among the elders of the land. (Prov. 31:23)

Right in the middle of this chapter in Proverbs, which describes a virtuous woman, is this one sentence about her husband. I believe that she is a big part of the reason her husband is known

Not Demonstrating Respect to Him

in the gates, the ruling place in the city. We don't know all of his qualities, so I am going to assume her actions help put him in such a position of respect. Let me tell you a story I heard:

> The mayor of a large city and his wife attended a banquet at a hotel. In order to avoid the rush of people after it was over, they left the back way and walked to their office. On the way, they passed a building under construction. One of the construction workers yelled out a greeting to the wife. She waved and continued walking with her husband. The mayor asked his wife who that man was. She replied that he had been her boyfriend at one time. Feeling rather proud, the mayor asked his wife, "Aren't you glad you married me? Because if you had married him, you would've been the wife of a construction worker." The mayor's wife replied, "No, the truth is, if I had married him, *he* would be mayor."

This story illustrates the point that, behind every successful man, there is a woman. I also believe that behind almost every failure of a man, there is a woman. When a man feels respected, he can accomplish so much. As women, we have such an ability to be a great influence in our husband's life. We were created to be the influence. What an awesome position God has given us!

If we want our husband to rise to the position God has for him, we need to be an encouragement. When you talk about your husband, make sure you are speaking in an edifying way. It is very hard for me to be around a woman who is constantly whining and complaining about her husband. My husband has weaknesses. I'm not blind to them or denying them, but I'm not calling my girlfriends and griping, either. I am doing my best to speak uplifting words about him, because I want him to rise to his potential, and I know I have a part to play in that. How are you talking about your husband to your friends and coworkers? We demonstrate respect not only by how we talk *about* him, but also in how we talk *to* him. We need to realize his position as head of the home and talk to him that way.

In Proverbs, chapter 31, we are encouraged to open our mouth with wisdom and kindness. *Kindness* literally means "loyalty." The words we use should show loyalty to our husband. When you're loyal to someone, you demonstrate that you're on the same team. A surefire way for me to start a fight with Philip is for me to come into a conversation, attacking with both guns blazing! (I always carry at least one!) What Proverbs is asking us to do, is approach our husband as if we are on the same team. Philip is not my enemy. (No matter how many times it has felt like it.) He and I should be on the

Not Demonstrating Respect to Him

same team, fighting a common enemy—not each other. Look at your heart: Do you secretly feel that you are on the opposite team from your husband? Begin to change that. Demonstrate respect by working together to overcome a problem. Demonstrate respect by being loyal.

How you talk to him is so important. A woman I know came to me for advice about an explosive situation with her husband. In the middle of some marital difficulties, she told her husband she had decided to spend a few days alone in prayer and fasting and that she did not want to answer the phone or to be with anyone, including friends. Not surprisingly, the husband, who felt like she was demanding something (she was), got angry and resentful. I applauded the woman's desire to spend time with God. But I smacked her (not really) for how she handled her desire, which was probably from God. She did not demonstrate respect to the man whom God had put as head of her home. Because she demanded something from him instead of asking, he pulled away and became resentful. I suggested that she go back to her husband, apologize for the way she spoke to him, and ask for what she needed in a respectful, honoring way. I encouraged her to say something like this: "Honey, I am so sorry for the way I was demanding. I know that wasn't respectful. Please forgive me. [This is called "eating humble pie" and is

HERS

33

often necessary.] I am really feeling overwhelmed right now and know that I am not able to give to you all I should. What would you think if I were to take a couple of days to fast and pray so that I can get my strength back and just get refreshed by God?"

She must have said something like this, because her husband's response totally changed. When she went to him as if they were members of the same team—who both wanted the best for each other—he responded with love and support. He even offered to get her a hotel room and take any phone messages for her while she was away. He offered to support her in any way necessary. When we are respectful, showing loyalty and demonstrating honor, great things happen.

The key here is in showing respect—by asking about an issue rather than telling what you are going to do or demanding that something be done. One of the turning points for my friend was that she asked her husband, "*What do you think* if I take a couple of days?" She asked him for his input. That opened the door to his heart. Many times on the way home from church with my husband, I will have an opinion about something I saw in the service. I have learned to handle this most delicately! I used to just blast forth with my opinion, assuming my husband wanted to hear it. When I did this, an invisible wall went up, and he didn't hear a thing I said. I complained to God about

Not Demonstrating Respect to Him

this, and the Lord assured me that what I had been trying to tell my husband was good, but that I was going about it in a very disrespectful way. And then He told me that He was holding me responsible for how I communicated my thoughts and opinions. He said this was my problem, not my husband's. I realized I needed to do something different if I wanted my husband to hear and receive what I believe was God-given inspiration. The next time I had an opinion about the way something should go in church, I asked Philip if I could share it with him.

Now, in spite of my weaknesses, my husband does know that God sent me to him to help him, and so he does want to hear what I have to say. When I asked, he said yes, and then I shared whatever nugget of truth I needed to. He was grateful, and then we talked about the situation. There have been times, however, when I have asked if he wanted to know what I thought and he said, "No, not now. We'll talk later." I was OK with that. We need to give our husband the freedom to say no, and not get resentful about it. Because my husband has seen the fruit of my comments and because he knows I have a real relationship with God and that my comments aren't necessarily just my opinion, but can also be God-given direction, he now asks for my thoughts and input regularly. This is because I don't force them on him. I respect his position enough

DUMB THINGS SHE DOES . . .

to ask. So did Queen Esther, and because she treated her husband with respect, she saved a nation.

In the Book of Esther we read that Esther became queen, basically because she won a beauty pageant. But she proved to have far more than her beauty going for her. Soon after she was made queen, she found out that her husband's right-hand man, Haman, had devised a plot to kill all of the Jews. Esther, herself a Jew, realized that she needed to do something. In fact, her cousin Mordecai suggested that for this cause she was made queen. First she asked all the Jews to pray. And then, rather than barging in to see her husband, the king, and demanding that something be done about Haman, she invited him to a feast. At the feast, Esther made sure she looked beautiful and that the food was great. At this first feast, she didn't ask anything of the king except that he come back to another banquet. Timing is everything! At this second feast, the king asked Esther what her petition was. She asked him to spare her life, telling him that Haman was plotting to kill all of the Jews, including herself. The king was outraged and had Haman killed, and then as king he provided a way for the Jews to defend themselves.

Because Esther handled the situation in a godly fashion, not only was her life and the lives of thousands of Jews spared, but also many of the Gentiles were converted. When we begin

Not Demonstrating Respect to Him

to demonstrate respect to our husband, not only will he be changed, not only will our relationship be strengthened, but we also will be an example of God's love to all of those watching.

Perhaps you are feeling frustrated because you feel your husband doesn't deserve respect. Don't despair! Find one good thing he does (there should be at least one—after all, you did marry him) and honor him for that. Change how you speak to him, and I believe you will see the results.

> **When you demonstrate respect to him, he will accomplish great things.**

CHAPTER THREE

TRYING TO FIX HIM—
NOT THAT HE DOESN'T NEED A GOOD FIXING!

I COULD HARDLY WAIT to marry Philip for a few reasons (one of which had to do with having been celibate for a long time). Another reason was that he needed some "fixing," and I was just the girl to do it. Most of us can hardly wait to marry the guy so that we can start changing him. We don't mean anything wrong by our attempts to change him; the relationship is just so important to us that we want to help it in whatever way possible.

DUMB THINGS SHE DOES . . .

John Gray, in his book *Men Are from Mars; Women Are from Venus,* says,

> When we try to improve a man, he feels we are trying to fix him. The motto of most men is, "If it's not broken, don't fix it." So if we are trying to fix him, he is receiving the message that he is "broken."*

Then he starts acting "broken," which is not what we want! We don't realize that our loving attempts to help him are really disrespectful. (Remember, the Bible tells us that feeling respected is his number-one need.) We think we are just helping him grow and that he is resisting our attempt to improve him. (Actually, he calls it *nagging.*) We think he is unwilling to change. The truth is, he is resistant to changing because he believes he is not being respected. When a man feels respected, automatically he begins to grow.

Most of us want our husband to be the spiritual leader in our home. Being the spiritual leader is one of his God-ordained roles. However, we can be a help or a hindrance. I have had women coming to me frustrated because their husband isn't fulfilling this role. Sometimes after listening to them for a while,

---

* John Gray, Ph.D., *Men Are from Mars, Women Are from Venus* (New York, NY: Harper Collins, 1992) p. 20.

Trying to Fix Him

I ask them, "How can your husband lead if you already are? If you want him to sit on the throne, you have to get off." If your husband feels like you are Mrs. Know-It-All or Mrs. Bible-Answer-Woman (and if that is how you are coming across), then he will not step up, because then he would risk being wrong—and men hate that. If you want him to begin taking leadership, start asking him questions: "Honey, what do you think that scripture means?" "What does the Bible say about . . . ?" "How should we pray with the children?"

Even if you have an answer, let him do the talking, and you be quiet. Don't let him get away with taking the backseat in your family's spiritual life—it's too important. The Bible does tell us in 1 Peter 3:1,

> Wives, be submissive to your own husband that even if some do not obey the word, they, without a word, may be won by the conduct of their wives.

It is hard for me to believe that by actually being quiet I can accomplish more than with my many brilliant words, but that is what the scripture says. If our husbands are not obeying the Word in some area, they will change by observing us, not by our taking over and doing the job, but rather by our quietly encouraging them and by our not being critical.

DUMB THINGS SHE DOES . . .

We all want our husband to spend what we consider to be an appropriate amount of time with our children. What I've seen, however, is that while they are with the children, we offer all sorts of "suggestions" about how they should do things. When my son, Jordan, was young, my husband offered to stay with him while I ran some errands. When I got back, I noticed the diaper was on backward—the little tape tabs were in the back. I quickly pointed this out to my husband and gave him an un-asked-for diapering lesson. As time passed, I began to notice that Philip was not offering to change Jordan's diaper very much. I realized what I had done and began to back off. Because, really, what does it matter if the diaper's on backward or upside down, as long as it's doing its job? And so what if Dad feeds the children junk food the night he's got them? Let him be the dad and spend time with them the way he wants.

I had a friend who complained to me that when her husband did the laundry, he put the towels and the sheets in the same load (as if this was a major crime). I would be excited if my husband knew where the washing machine was! I suggested to her that if she ever wanted him to do laundry again, she shouldn't complain, but rather, encourage and be grateful.

I am not quite sure how my husband managed to drive himself around for the thirty-one years before he met me. Once we

Trying to Fix Him

were married, I began to "fix" his driving, telling him what streets to take, the quickest way to get somewhere, and stomping my foot on the invisible brake pedal on my side of the car whenever he got too close to another car. When God began dealing with me about showing respect to my husband by not trying to fix him, it affected many areas of our life. I knew I had to give up my backseat driving. (I was actually allowed to sit in the front seat after a while!) I also knew it would be tough.

One day we were coming home from church on a route we had traveled hundreds of times. This time, I was determined to be silent, no matter how hard it was. Sure enough, as we came up to the freeway's off-ramp where we needed to exit, my husband sailed right on past it. I bit my tongue as we drove, and drove, and drove miles past our destination. Finally, Philip snapped out of whatever dazed state he had been in and asked, "Where in the world are we?"

I calmly said, "Woodland Hills" (which was the next town from ours).

We both laughed, but I learned a valuable lesson. (Philip did too.) Actually, he frequently asks me to help in finding a certain location, but I now do it with an entirely different spirit.

Most men don't usually leave their wife for someone prettier or for someone with more money, but rather, for some woman who respects him, some woman who thinks he "hung the moon." I remember talking to a woman whose husband had just left her. (This obviously was not the best choice for him to make.) She was complaining that he had left her for "some bimbo who thinks he's just wonderful." She proudly told me that *she* hadn't seen him through rose-colored glasses; *she* had stood up to him and had challenged him often. *She* hadn't seen him as some sort of superhero as his new girlfriend did. I actually felt bad for her because her pride was going to be a lonely companion in the years to come. Men need to feel respected. Your husband is looking to be someone's hero. Why not let him be yours? Here's a story to illustrate that point:

> Deep inside every man there is a hero or knight in shining armor. More than anything, he wants to succeed in serving and protecting the woman he loves. When he feels trusted, he is able to tap into this noble part of himself. He becomes more caring. When he doesn't feel trusted, he loses some of his aliveness and energy, and after a while, he can stop caring.
>
> Imagine a knight in shining armor traveling through the countryside. Suddenly he hears a woman crying out in distress. In an instant he comes alive. Urging his horse to a

Trying to Fix Him

gallop, he races to her castle, where she is trapped by a dragon. The noble knight pulls out his sword and slays the dragon.

As the gates open, he is welcomed and celebrated by the family of the princess and the townspeople. He is invited to live in the town and is acknowledged as a hero. He and the princess fall in love.

A month later, the noble knight goes off on another trip. On his way back, he hears his beloved princess crying out for help. Another dragon has attacked the castle. When the knight arrives, he pulls out his sword to slay the dragon.

Before he swings, the princess cries out from the tower, "Don't use your sword, use this noose. It will work better." She throws him the noose and motions to him instructions about how to use it. He hesitantly follows her instructions. The dragon dies and everyone rejoices.

At the celebration dinner, the knight feels he didn't really do anything. Somehow, because he used her noose and didn't use his sword, he doesn't quite feel worthy of the town's trust and admiration. After the event, he is slightly depressed and forgets to shine his armor.

A month later, he goes on yet another trip. As he leaves with his sword, the princess reminds him to be careful and tells him to take the noose. On his way home, he sees yet another dragon attacking the castle. This time he rushes forward with his sword but hesitates, thinking maybe he should

Dumb Things She Does . . .

use the noose. In that moment of hesitation, the dragon breathes fire and burns his right arm. In confusion, he looks up and sees his princess waving from the castle window. "Use the poison," she yells. "The noose doesn't work."

She throws him the poison, which he pours into the dragon's mouth, and the dragon dies. Everyone rejoices and celebrates, but the knight feels ashamed.

A month later, he goes on another trip. As he leaves with his sword, the princess reminds him to be careful and to bring the noose and the poison. He is annoyed by her suggestions but brings them just in case.

This time on his journey he hears another woman in distress. As he rushes to her call, his depression is lifted and he feels confident and alive. But as he draws his sword to slay the dragon, he again hesitates. He wonders, should I use my sword, the noose, or the poison? What would the princess say?

For a moment he is confused. But then he remembers how he had felt before he knew the princess, back in the days when he only carried a sword. With a burst of renewed confidence he throws off the noose and poison, and charges the dragon with his trusted sword. He slays the dragon and the townspeople rejoice.

The knight in shining armor never returned to his princess. He stayed in this new village and lived happily ever

Trying to Fix Him

after. He eventually married, but only after making sure his new partner knew nothing about nooses and poisons.

Remembering that within every man is a knight in shining armor is a powerful metaphor to help you remember a man's primary needs. Although a man may appreciate caring and assistance. Sometimes, too much of it will lessen his confidence or turn him off.*

Our job is not to fix or change our husband. We are not their teacher. That is the job of the Holy Spirit. (Not that there weren't times I didn't try to be my husband's holy spirit.) We are to be the influence, letting our heart, character, and integrity speak for themselves. Come on, women, we *can* do this! Find a girlfriend who is also committed to respecting her husband as you are, and encourage each other. Help each other in your pursuit of a wonderful marriage.

> **There are plenty of things in your life to fix; your husband is not one of them.**

* *Men Are from Mars, Women Are from Venus*, p. 138.

CHAPTER FOUR

NOT GETTING INVOLVED IN WHAT HE'S DOING—
HE REALLY DOES WANT YOU THERE

IT IS GOOD FOR EACH OF US to have our own interests. In fact, it is very important. Outside of my relationship with the Lord, my husband should be the biggest part of my life. However, he is not the *only* part. That's too much pressure to put on anyone. I should have my own friends, my own interests, and my own goals that all contribute to making me a fun and interesting person. And at the same time, I can't be so busy with "my life" that Philip and I become separate, each doing our own thing. It is important to share some areas of life.

My husband is a pastor, and when I met him, while he hadn't started the church yet, I knew that he would be involved in ministry. When we made the decision to get married, he assured me that he didn't have any preconceived ideas about what a pastor's wife should do. He said that he just wanted me to be his wife and that God's purpose would become evident. He wasn't expecting me to play the piano or sing (good thing!), which is what I thought was the traditional role for a pastor's wife. So, when we first started in ministry, I served in many areas, but was always focused on discovering the ministry that *God* had for me. As I grew in God and as His purpose for my life became clearer, I began to minister alongside my husband. I began teaching more and more, and we truly began to share more of the load. Teaching isn't necessarily the role every pastor's wife should fill, but it was a role suited for me. We now share the work and the vision of the ministry.

If your husband is an auto mechanic, you don't necessarily need to know how to fix a car, but you should know something about what he does. If your husband is a computer designer or technician, you don't have to understand everything about computers (I certainly don't!), but you should respect his job enough to be able to carry on a conversation, using some computer language. If your husband is a physician or an attorney and

Not Getting Involved in What He's Doing

belongs to various associations, attend some meetings and functions with him. Find some way to share his job with him, even though you aren't called to have the same job.

Sharing some of the same interests is also important. Philip *really* likes basketball. Before I met him, I knew what a basketball looked like and the difference between offense and defense, but that was about it (despite the fact that I began my college career at Duke University, which is a big basketball school). Rather than resenting the fact that my husband is a basketball maniac, I decided to join him. I now go to the games with him. In fact, I actually cheer much louder than he does. I know a lot of the players, what teams are doing well, and a lot of the basketball lingo. I knew I had it really bad when during the basketball playoffs, I had the game on the television and Philip wasn't even home!

What is your husband involved in? What is an interest he has that you can share, at least on some level? Read some of the same books. The kind of books that Philip likes aren't necessarily my favorite, but I do read some of them. We have great discussions, and it demonstrates to him that I am interested in him, what he thinks and what he does. At the same time, over the years, he has shown a lot of interest in my pursuits and desires. (Like sitting through romantic, girl-type movies with me—not just once, either!) While we each have different interests that make us who we are, it is important to find areas of our life that we can share.

> # Share the work,
> # and share the fun!

Chapter Five

Being a Dream Stealer—
C'mon, Cheer Him on Girls!

Most people, including your husband, are surrounded by negativity all day. Some of the negativity comes from outside influences, but some comes from inside, springing up from his own self-doubts. He can be bombarded with comments, such as "That'll never work!" "No, you can't do that." *I don't have what it takes. I'm not qualified to do this.* You and I need to be his encourager—the one who says, "You can do it!

What a great idea!" We need to be the one who reminds him what Philippians 1:6 says:

> . . . be confident of this very thing, that he who has begun a good work in you will complete it. . . .

I was a cheerleader in high school; maybe some of you were too. Now, the social ramifications that go with that position today might not be so great, but the honor of being someone's cheerleader is. We should all be our husband's cheerleader! He needs it, and he won't get it from most other people. A cheerleader is someone who speaks encouragement.

The word *encourage* means "to put courage in." Courage means facing danger in spite of fear. As we encourage, we are saying, "Keep going; keep doing right; you'll get it!" When my son was ten months old, he decided he was ready to walk. I propped him up against a wall, and my husband was ready with the video camera. He took one little step and then fell on his diapered bottom. I cheered loudly, clapping and telling him what a great job he did. I stood him back up and he began the process again. He took a few faltering steps before he fell. I hugged him, told him how smart he was, and we started again. Now, did I want him to walk like this forever? No.

Being a Dream Stealer

I was actually hoping that, sooner or later, he could string more than two wobbly steps together. But in the meantime, I encouraged every step he made.

As wives, we need to encourage every step our husband is taking in the right direction. He may not be doing something exactly how you want him to, but encourage him along the way. If he is reading books about, and generally working on, his relationship with you, encourage any good thing you see. Instead of complaining about the kind of flowers he brought, thank him!

Watch being critical and impatient, expecting him to get it right immediately. You and I don't always get it right either, so let's dish out the encouragement that we ourselves need. How many of us have ever made a mistake? All of us. Wouldn't it be great if our spouse was cheering us on as we picked ourselves up and started again?

We serve the God of the second (and third, and fourth, and fifth, etc.) chance. Make sure you are giving your husband more than one chance to accomplish whatever is in his heart!

> ## Applaud his dreams and his attempts to reach them.

Chapter Six

Not Understanding Your Role—
Take a Deep Breath before Reading This One!

J UST HEARING THE WORD *SUBMISSION* used to make me cringe. It was like fingernails being run down a chalkboard. *Aagh*! I was raised, probably like many of you, in a generation that was encouraged to challenge authority, to submit to no one—especially not a woman to a man. Helen Reddy sang, "I am woman, hear me roar . . . ," and it was an appropriate theme song. The feminists were telling me—a well-educated, well-traveled woman—to focus on a chosen career and not to let a family or husband cloud the way. I was encouraged to believe that a job would meet most of my needs. If I still wanted a family, I could do that later—there was always time. While I am grateful for the benefits brought about by the feminists in the workplace and in society, they did not teach me accurately about how to relate to a man and be a part of a husband-wife team. I didn't learn that my family should be my number-one priority in order for it to be a successful one.

In both Ephesians 5:22 and 1 Peter 3:1, God is telling me, as a married woman, my role is to yield to and submit to my husband and to his position as leader. (Those of you, who are grimacing right now, take a deep breath and try to finish the chapter. It won't be that painful.) Just as on a ship there is only one captain, so in a marriage there is just one head. (A two-headed anything is a monster!) The captain is not more valuable than any other person on the ship. The title merely defines his position. In fact, any problems on the ship ultimately are his responsibility. Your husband is not more valuable than you are. By making him the head, God is merely establishing order.

On a sports team, there is just one head coach. Imagine the confusion on the team if more then one person was giving the players direction. The coach certainly isn't more important than the players. His job is to recognize the strengths of the different players and to let them do their stuff. Phil Jackson's job, as head

Not Understanding Your Role

coach of the Chicago Bulls, was to discover the strengths of Michael Jordan, Scottie Pippin, and Dennis Rodman and to direct them to work together and to overcome weaknesses. He did not try to control Dennis Rodman (who could?) and turn him into another Michael Jordan. He recognized the defensive strengths of Rodman and encouraged those. My husband's job as "coach" in our marriage, is to encourage and lead in such a way that my strengths shine. It didn't start out this way. In the beginning, he wasn't a good leader, and I was busy trying to be the coach. Our home was a mess! But as he learned about leading, and I began to trust and yield to his leadership, God's peace filled our home.

You and I need to make a paradigm shift. We are not giving up who we are or our strengths, but we are using them in a way that will help the team. Submission is not being subservient; it is not being a mousy doormat, which is what most of us think. Submission is using our powerful, God-given role in a relationship. It is being our husband's number-one influence. Submission is not a mystery. It is not a feeling. It is a decision of the will. It is an awesome act of faith that will move the hand of God.

By yielding to my husband, I am ultimately putting my faith in the One who created him, to work things out. This is not an easy task, because most of the time and in most situations, I would rather be in charge. But I have learned to love the wonderful role God has given me. I have learned the honor of being the influence in my husband's life. I am a strong, wise, talkative woman, and I offer godly influence in my husband's life. My husband is not intimidated by my strengths, and he doesn't stifle the woman I am.

Submission is not yielding to abuse or being passive and quiet. It is taking action in a way that brings honor and respect to the relationship. Submission is merely (actually, there's no *merely* about it) putting into practice what I've talked about in the previous chapters. Submission is respecting your husband and speaking to him in a way that demonstrates that. Submission is trusting him and *not* trying to fix him. Submission is adapting yourself to your husband and getting involved in some areas of his life. Submission is being your husband's number-one cheerleader.

While I am challenging you married women, submission and its rewards are indeed for all believers. Ephesians 5:22, 33 tells us that, as Christians, we are to be submitted to one another. And in 1 Peter 3:13–21, we are also asked to submit to ruling authorities as well as to our employers. As an employee,

Not Understanding Your Role

your job is to support your boss and to make him or her look good, regardless of whether you are male or female.

Shanelle, who is now a good friend of mine, came to our church about ten years ago while she was attending the University of Southern California. She came to a Sunday-morning service, received Jesus, and began her journey of walking with Him. She is a very intelligent woman and soon graduated with an engineering degree. After she had been working for a few months at a job she had prayed to get, she came to me, complaining about her boss. She claimed that she knew more than he did. He was too hard to work for and didn't listen to her ideas. She didn't think she could take it anymore. I agreed with her, that it sounded like a difficult situation, and then asked her if she wanted some help in dealing with it—to which she replied yes. Our conversation basically went something like this:

"Shanelle, do you believe God gave you this job?"

"Yes."

"Do you think there are things you need to learn from this company?"

"Yes, I do."

"What do you think your job as an employee is?"

"Well, I guess it's to support my boss and do good work."

"OK, are you doing that?"

"Well, he makes it so hard."

"Who said growth was easy? Your job as his employee is to learn from him, to be a good representative of him, to adapt yourself to his requirements, and to be faithful to do good work—that is, if you want promotion."

She assured me she did want to advance in the company and that she was willing to try it God's way. It wasn't an easy task, but she humbled herself and stopped seeing herself as superior. Just like it says in Matthew 11:33, she sought first God's Kingdom—His order—and all sorts of things have been added to her life. In a short span of years, she was promoted to the vice-president level of her company, where she was the highest-paid woman executive. And even when her level of authority increased, she remained submitted to those in a position over her. She has continued to find favor within the company and with her clients all over the world—all because she took a step of faith and yielded to that first boss years ago. Now I believe, as a direct result of her faithfulness in this job, she has been offered a position as an officer in the United Nations, where she will have global influence. Praise God! When we honor His established authority, He is always faithful to bless us. She took the same step of faith you and I must take if we want to see God's blessing in our families.

Not Understanding Your Role

I thank God daily, not only for saving me, but also for teaching me about His order. God has an amazing, awesome place for you and me if we are courageous enough to walk in it. Let's give it a try, shall we? The rewards are precious.

> **Yielding to authority is an act of faith and will always produce blessings.**

Dumb Things We Both Do . . .

Chapter One

Not Forgiving—
Go Ahead, Say "I'm Sorry"

I'M SURE IT'S TAKEN YOU A WHILE, but by now you have probably realized that your spouse isn't perfect. And if you are waiting for that spouse to one day be the perfect husband or the perfect wife, you are in for a very long wait. We are all going to make mistakes—some big, some little—as we live out our marriages. I have learned that marriages are built on forgiveness, not on perfection. We need to be quick to forgive each other.

Ephesians 4:32 tells us that we need to forgive each other just as Christ forgave us. That scripture really puts it into perspective. Who am I to hold on to grudges or bitterness against my husband, when Jesus has forgiven me for so much more? Mark 11:25, 26 says it like this:

> And whenever you stand praying, if you have anything against anyone, forgive him, that your Father in heaven may also forgive you your trespasses. But if you do not forgive, neither will your Father in heaven forgive your trespasses.

Forgiveness is serious business. I believe it is a life-and-death issue. The reason we are told, in verse 25, to stop praying and to forgive first, is because we can't pray effectively if we have an unforgiving spirit. I can't be in fellowship with God with unforgiveness in my heart. The prayer God wants to hear is the prayer forgiving the one who offended. If we hold unforgiveness in our heart, no matter how justified we feel, according to the scripture in Matthew, our sins won't be forgiven us. Since sin is what separates us from God (Rom. 3:23), by holding on to unforgiveness, we are separated from Him. We don't want that. As we forgive, we are forgiven.

Forgiveness is pardoning someone. It is letting go of the resentment. Forgiveness is not necessarily forgetting. When God said He would remember our sins no more (Jer. 31:34), He was saying that He would never use our past against us. Forgetting may be the result of forgiveness, but it is never the means.

Not Forgiving

Forgiveness can be difficult for us because it pulls against our concept of justice. We want revenge for offenses suffered. (Oh, sometimes we won't admit it, but we do!) We want God to bless them with a lighting bolt! You may ask, "Why should I let them off the hook?" That's the problem: you're hooked. Or we'll say, "But you don't understand how much they hurt me!" But don't you see? They are still hurting you. You are still living the betrayal, the offense, whatever the crime. You don't forgive someone for their sake; you do it for your sake. Your need to forgive isn't an issue between you and your spouse; it's between you and God. No matter what the offense, God requires you to forgive.

Forgiveness is a choice, a decision of your will. Don't wait until you feel like forgiving to begin the process; you'll never get there. Feelings take time to heal after the choice to forgive has been made.

There have been times when Philip has hurt my feelings by something he has said or done or hasn't done. He's usually aware my feelings are hurt. He would then say, "I'm sorry your feelings are hurt," *not* "I'm sorry that I hurt your feelings. I was wrong," which is, of course, what I want him to say. But I have realized that my forgiving him is between God and me. By holding on to that grudge, I'm only hurting my relationship with God. And I have also learned that I need to forgive, whether or not Philip says, "I'm sorry." (Men, now would be a good time to practice saying "I'm sorry" out loud. Go ahead. For some reason it seems to be harder for you guys.) My forgiving Philip is not based on whether or not he apologizes. Now, of course, he should, and so should I. In fact, we both have gotten so good at saying "I'm sorry," we say it no matter whose fault it is. The movie *Love Story* popularized the statement, "Love means never having to say you're sorry." Well, I think love is being the first to say you're sorry.

When we hold on to grudges, we begin to withdraw from each other and withhold affection, which will ultimately destroy the relationship. Marriages are about forgiving—daily. If you find that, right now, you are feeling separate from your spouse, I would wager there is some unresolved offense between the two of you. Approach your spouse humbly and without blaming. Describe how you are feeling rather than pointing your finger at him or her.

The ultimate betrayal in a marriage is adultery. If a spouse commits adultery, the spouse who was betrayed has a few choices. First, they can choose to forgive. Even though they are angry, they ultimately choose to forgive the betrayal, perhaps getting counseling and working on reconciling the relationship, and all the while, remaining committed to forgive.

Not Forgiving

Secondly, the betrayed spouse can leave. In Matthew 19:9 Jesus says, "And I say to you, whoever divorces his wife, except for sexual immorality, and marries another, commits adultery; and whoever marries her who is divorced commits adultery."

Most people I have met who have been betrayed by adultery, don't really do either. They decide to stay, but instead of forgiving, they begin to withhold affection and love. They make the spouse who sinned feel guilty by constantly using the sin against them. While there hasn't been an actual divorce, there has been an emotional one. The betrayed one is trying to punish the offender. They don't want to leave the marriage because that wouldn't be "Christian." Somehow in their mind, staying seems to be a more Christian approach, even though they are angry, withhold love, and are bitter for years. I don't pretend to know the pain involved in this kind of betrayal. What I do know is that whether the betrayed one stays or goes, he or she still must forgive.

I read an article years ago about a couple who was in marriage counseling. The wife was complaining to the counselor about her husband's "little black book." The counselor, thinking she knew what was in the black book, understood why the wife would be upset. The wife then went on to say that, in this black book, her husband had written down every mistake she had made since the beginning of their marriage, and she just couldn't take it anymore.

When I read this I became furious on the wife's behalf, wanting to go after that self-righteous husband. After I had finished muttering about the husband, I heard the Lord say quietly in my spirit, *You do that too.* I quickly told God that I did no such thing, that I had not written down my husband's mistakes. And then I heard Him say again, *No, you don't write them down on paper, but you are keeping a record of them in you heart.* I realized that He was right. I had been keeping track of all the times Philip had offended me. I repented right then and made the decision to never again keep a record of my husband's wrongdoings. No more keeping score. I was going to be so ready to forgive that I would begin forgiving even before the offense was finished (at least, that's my goal—to be so full of forgiveness).

In the marriage relationship, we each have specific roles to fill. Husbands, your job is not an easy one, so wives give him a break. He is not going to get it right all the time. Forgive the failures. Cheer the attempts. And husbands, we too, have a difficult job. There will be times when we blow it, when we aren't respectful or yielded. Please be quick to forgive and encourage us to try again. Demonstrate forgiveness and love anyway.

Not Forgiving

Because forgiveness is not an easy task, we won't be able to be successful unless we each have a real, growing relationship with God. Keep your heart softened toward your heavenly Father, and He will keep yours softened to those around you.

Be a great forgiver. The task is difficult, but not impossible. You can do it!

> **Be the first to say I'm sorry; don't keep a record of offenses.**

Chapter Two

Not Fighting Fair—
Yes, There Are Rules!

"You started it!"
"No, you did!"
"No, you did when you changed your mind."
"Why do you always blame me?"
"I'm outta here!" *Slam!*

Sounds like a couple of children fighting, doesn't it? Actually, I've heard words like this between adults. No matter how strong the marriage, conflicts will arise. Learning how to deal with them is crucial. Resolving conflicts can strengthen a marriage greatly.

I had a discussion one time with a woman who said she and her husband never argued; conflicts never arose in their marriage. As I spent time with them, I noticed this was basically true. I also noticed a total lack of intimacy, honesty, and a superficial level of communication that would eventually lead to trouble. Resolving conflicts opens lines of communication, relieves tension, solves problems, and airs differences—all of which are important in strengthening a marriage.

In an argument, oftentimes one or both of you are angry. Anger isn't the problem; it's what happens *when* you're angry that can be problematic. According to Ephesians 4:26, it is possible to be angry and not sin. How do you handle your anger? Do you yell, hit, or call each other names? That's abuse, and that's a problem. Do you let your anger push you toward resolving the conflict, or do you attack with it? It is important to learn to manage your anger in resolving conflicts, or you will have bigger problems on your hands.

In any conflict, make sure to stay focused on the issue being brought up. Don't bring out a list of all the things your spouse has done over the years. Unrelated issues are off-limits. Don't blame, accuse, or use words, such as *never* and *always*. It's better to make the discussion about your personal feelings than it is to point a finger. Use statements, such as "When ——— happens,

Not Fighting Fair

I feel ———— ." Or "I need ———— ." Or "What would make me feel better is ———— ."

Using phrases, that begin with "You should" or "You need to" or "You always" will only escalate the conflict. Try to remain calm and logical. You'll get better results if you can express yourself honestly and directly.

Pick your arguments carefully. Don' fight over every little thing. That becomes exhausting and minimizes the issues that are really important to you.

Don't start resolving a conflict late at night when you're both tired and emotions are frazzled. It's better to resolve the issue when you are both at your best physically. Unless anger has escalated to rage and you are incapable of managing yourself, then don't leave the room. Commit to continue until the conflict has been resolved, peace is restored, or you have agreed to work it out at another time. It is childish to walk out, slamming doors. Adults resolve issues—seeking peace.

Pray. Pray before beginning a discussion that you think could turn into an argument, pray during an argument, and pray after. Pray whenever you can. Pray that the words you use will not be careless or hurtful. Pray that the devil won't gain any ground in your marriage, and that God's will is done. Prayer brings God's presence into the situation, which is what will bring the resolution.

As a general rule, don't argue in front of your children unless you are willing to make up in front of them. It is important for our children to see how we resolve conflicts, not just how we start them. However, I would set very narrow limits on what my children see or hear. There was a couple I knew whose child watched them fight—not resolve conflicts, but fight. The child heard them yelling and calling each other names. If you haven't learned how to resolve conflicts in a godly way, don't fight in front of anyone, and please get some help from a counselor. Children are helped when they see a mature person resolve a conflict. They are destroyed when they witness the two people, who should be providing security, yelling and attacking each other.

Conflict resolution is a skill that takes practice, humility, and the presence of God. Be willing to take the time needed; be willing to be wrong; and be willing to pray for God's direction and wisdom. You can do it!

In a calm manner, focus on the issue at hand, praying for God's direction in resolving the conflict.

CHAPTER THREE

NOT UNDERSTANDING OUR DIFFERENCES—
VIVA LA DIFFERENCE!

WE ARE EACH UNIQUELY CREATED with different strengths, different abilities, and different personalities. While, as Christians, our goal is eventually to look like Jesus, we each have different strengths and weaknesses that need to be dealt with along the journey. In spite of the differences, we are called by God to love one another. John 13:34–35 says,

> A new commandment I give to you, that you love one another, as I have loved you, that you also love one another. By

this all will know that you are my disciples, if you have love for one another.

The way we will touch the world is not by the Jesus T-shirts we wear, not by the fish emblem on our bumper, not by the big Bible we carry, nor the Bible verses we can quote. All of these are good, but Jesus said, in the Gospel of John, that we will impact the world by how we demonstrate our love for each other. God could have made it easy to love each other by giving us all the same personalities, but He didn't, so we have to rejoice in the differences and love each other anyway. Carl Rogers said it like this,

> When I walk on the beach to watch the sunset, I do not call out, "A little more orange over to the right please," or, "Would you mind giving us less purple in the back?" No, I enjoy the always different sunsets as they are. We do well to do the same with people we love.*

The reason it is important to understand the differences in our personalities, is so that we can function more effectively as a team. In 1 Corinthians, chapter 12, we are told that while we

---

* Carl Rogers, *Illustrations Unlimited.* James Hewitt, ed. (Wheaton, IL: Tyndale House, 1988) p. 338.

Not Understanding Our Differences

are a part of the same body, we each have different functions in the body. Husband, your wife is not you. She won't think or act like you on most occasions. Wife, your husband is not you. He won't respond the same way you would most of the time.

Organizations all over the country are administering personality profiles to their employees, so that employers can better place people in jobs where they would flourish, and so the employees will function better together. There are many different types of profiles, although they are all basically similar. Hippocrates, hundreds of years ago, developed a system that is helpful and easy to understand. He said there are basically four major personality types.

Every person probably has one dominant personality type and a secondary one, so the combinations are multiplied. No one is put into a box. There is no right personality. No personality is better than another and each has strengths and weaknesses. Remember, we are learning this to better discover where we fit in the body of Christ and how to more effectively love our spouse.

The first personality type I'll talk about is the sanguine. These people are usually the easiest to recognize when walking into a room, because everything about them is moving: their arms, their hands, and their mouth! These people are excited, energetic, spontaneous, and fun-loving. These are the party-waiting-to-happen people, and they can prevent many dull moments. They are outgoing and love to be with people. They can get any project started with a bang. On the other hand, they are not great at finishing those projects. They can forget obligations and can be undisciplined. They often speak without thinking. (Their motto being Ready. Fire. Aim!) Emotionally they need a lot of attention, affection, and approval.

Another personality type is the melancholy. These people are analytical, and like things done perfectly. (Whiteout and spell-check were invented for them!) They are schedule-oriented and compassionate. They tend to be talented and creative, often genius-prone. Their clothes are enduring (rather than trendy), precise, and have few (if any) wrinkles. (They don't usually like linen.) They can also be hard to please, negative, and depressed over imperfections. Emotionally they need sensitivity, support, and silence.

Quite often these two marry each other. (We did.) I'm the sanguine, and Philip is the melancholy. It doesn't get much more different than that. The great thing is, where I am weak, he is strong and vice-versa. However, initially it drove me nuts! He likes all of his "ducks in a row," and I wasn't even aware there

Not Understanding Our Differences

were ducks! I kept trying to make him wrong, thinking that he should have been more like me!

Our closet was an interesting place to work out our differences. His clothes were arranged very neatly. Shirts with short sleeves in one section, then shirts with long sleeves in another, then dark-colored trousers, light ones, then jeans, and then suits were in their own section. And of course the ties were placed on one spinning rack, and belts on another. Shoes were neatly arranged on shelves. It was an amazing masterpiece! My style of closet management came closer to the "if when I kicked my shoe off, it hit the doorframe, I called it put away" style. I'm sure that those of you who are melancholys are cringing at the thought of what I did. My husband did too. Gradually, I realized that his organizational skills were a definite strength. He could actually find his clothes in his closet! Rather than continue to call him picky, I let his strength influence my weakness. Now my closet, while it will never be quite as together as his, is vastly more organized. One time, in order to surprise my husband, I installed racks for my shoes. When he came home he was as excited as a melancholy could get. You'd have thought I'd given him a thousand dollars! He has also learned to value my outgoing nature. We meet more people and have more friends because I am such a people person. He likes being with me because I make things more fun. We have learned to value the differences in each other, helping each other overcome weaknesses so we will each be more Christlike.

The third personality type is the choleric. This person walks with purpose and focus, never forgetting why they were going from point A, to point B. (The sanguine would have stopped to talk to someone along the way, forgetting entirely about point B.) Cholerics can be great leaders, exude confidence, and excel in emergencies. They can see the whole picture and assume leadership where there is none. They can also be impatient and bossy. They have a hard time relaxing and may have a hard time saying I'm sorry. They also might run over people on the way to reach a goal. Emotionally they need loyalty, appreciation, and a sense of control.

The fourth personality type is the phlegmatic. These are the least obvious to identify. They are not extremely anything. They tend to be chameleon-like, capable of adapting in many circumstances. Their clothing is the most relaxed that is acceptable. They are easygoing, sympathetic, good listeners, and make great friends. They are the peacemakers. They can also be unenthusiastic, indecisive, lazy, and resistant to change. (It might

Not Understanding Our Differences

take a stick of dynamite to move them to something new.) Emotionally they need peace and quiet, and a lack of stress.

If these two marry each other, they will also have challenges. One wants to be on the go, conquering new goals, and the other wants to quietly do it how they've always done it. The choleric has to be careful not to run over the phlegmatic, but rather learn to appreciate the quiet strength that's offered. And the phlegmatic can learn to try something new and to go to new places.

Whether you have married someone who is very similar to you with a lot of the same strengths and weaknesses (scary thought) or someone quite different, it takes work to go from hating any differences, to understanding them, to valuing them. Learn to treasure how God made your spouse.

Don't expect your spouse to be like you. I don't expect Philip to be Mr. Social. I know that after he has been at a function for few hours, he's ready for some quiet time. I don't resent this about him, I just accept it. And at the same time, he doesn't resent my need for affection; he has learned to be good at giving it.

Don't hold on to weaknesses saying, "Well, that's just how God made me." Our goal is to be like Jesus, and we will be recognizing weaknesses and overcoming them all along the way. We need each other to get the job done.

Discover your unique personality and that of your spouse, and begin working together to form a stronger union.

> **Treasure the differences in each other, and let them bring strength to the relationship.**

CHAPTER FOUR

EXPECT A GREAT MARRIAGE TO JUST HAPPEN—
CINDERELLA WAS A FAIRY TALE!

OURS

I LOVED PHILIP. HE LOVED ME. Then we both said, "I do." I thought that was all it took to have a great marriage: love and a wedding ring. Boy, was I in for a shock after the first month! We all expect our physicians to have gone through years of school and residency in order to be good at what they do, and yet most of us expect to have a strong marriage without ever learning how. Wouldn't it be great if all universities required the students to take a Marriage 101 class? In the long run, that class would certainly prove more useful than the calculus class I took. But for those of us who missed the Marriage 101 class, there is hope!

One of the most important things to do in a marriage is to continue learning how to be a better spouse. It is vital that we continue to grow in our role as a husband or wife, because it is one we will have for a lifetime.

When looking through a microscope, scientists can tell a living organism from an inanimate one by observing any change. If, after a matter of time, there is no growth or change, the object is considered a dead one. It is the same with you and me as individuals and as part of a marriage.

It is important that we grow, both as individuals and as a part of a couple. As individuals, it's important that we be willing to learn new things and think new thoughts. We won't make it through life the way God intended us to, by thinking old thoughts. We need to meet new people, read new books, take new challenges, and set new goals. In other words, we need to be a lifelong student.

I read an article in *Parade* magazine a few years ago that told the story of a group of nuns who consistently lived to be over 100 years of age. Scientists went to their convent to study them and see what was different about how they lived. The scientists got permission to perform autopsies on the nuns who

Expect a Great Marriage to Just Happen

died. During the autopsies, they discovered something interesting. The brains of the nuns had many more connections between different points than most people's brains. These specific connections formed when the brain was learning something new. The scientists then found out, after speaking to some of the nuns, that this group of nuns was continually learning new things, right up until death. They were learning to speak new languages, work new machines, and read new books all the way into their nineties.

Because the brain was continually growing and being used, the nuns lived longer. You and I need to be the type of people who want to learn new things, not just so that our life will be longer, but so that it will be fuller. The growth that I make and the changes I embrace won't change who I am, but they will make me a better me.

As part of a marriage, we need to grow in a couple of ways. We need to be a student of our spouse, not only in learning their personality strengths and weaknesses, but also in learning their likes, dislikes, and needs. We need to learn about them, not to change them, but to know them, from the simple, to the more complex—from knowing their favorite food, to knowing what they need when they're hurting. Does he like some space to figure out a problem? Does she need you to listen to and hold her? Does he like surprises? Does she like everything planned out? What are your husbands dreams? What are your wife's fears? What is she looking forward to? What is he hoping for? The tricky part about this is you have to be willing and prepared for your spouse to grow and change just as you are doing. Their favorite cereal might change!

As part of a couple, we need to continually be learning about marriage. There are so many great books, tapes, and videos out there that are designed to strengthen you as a couple. I have shelves and shelves of them. I figure that being a wife is one role I will have for the rest of my life, and I want to continually improve at it.

Oftentimes people will come to me for some help in their marriage. I am always amazed when I find out that the couple hasn't read a book or listened to a tape on marriage. If they wanted to know how to build a car, they would study and read books on how to do it. Yet most people want to build a great marriage and aren't taking advantage of the great products available. There are conferences, seminars, and retreats available for you to attend. These will provide, not only great information, but also a boost that all marriages will enjoy. Please read books, listen to tapes, or go to a seminar. Your marriage will definitely benefit.

Another way to build a great marriage is to spend time with a couple who has been happily married for longer than you have. I

Expect a Great Marriage to Just Happen

qualified that statement with *happily*, because spending time with people who are down on marriage or negative about their spouse will not be helpful, to say the least. Just as first-time mothers learn from experienced mothers, so we can learn from couples who have been married longer. Find some couples you can spend time with and do it. Extend yourself. You will love the results.

Also, first-time mothers need to spend time with other first-time mothers, so that together they can help each other through all the new experiences that come with a baby. Likewise, it's important for us to spend time with couples who are at the same place as we are on the journey of life. There is no replacement for friends who will see you through the obstacles and rejoice with you over the victories. Your marriage will grow and be strengthened as you build relationships with other likeminded couples. Go for it!

Be committed to growing more as a person and as part of a marriage. Growth and change produce life.

CHAPTER FIVE

ONE LAST THING—
AND I DO MEAN THAT!

THANKS FOR TAKING THE TIME to read my little book. I hope that the title of this book is not offensive to anyone. I am certainly not saying that anyone of you is dumb! However, most of us have done at least one or two dumb things in our life.

My prayer is that you will take whatever you learned in these pages and put it to use in your marriage. Also I pray that you will continue to read books on men, women, and marriage. There are many wonderful books out there that God can use to propel your marriage to the next level.

And *please* take to the time to include God in your marriage. Spending time together praying and reading the Bible can be invaluable. As individuals we need to be building our own relationship with the Father, and we also need to be building our relationship with God as a couple. Perhaps you've seen the billboards that say, "The family that prays together, stays together." I would have to agree. Prayer brings in His presence, and where His presence is, there is joy, peace, and love. What marriage could survive without those? His presence can make all the difference in a marriage.

So, go on, get out there and build the strongest marriage possible.

> # The dumbest thing we could do is read a book like this and do nothing about it!

To order additional copies of

Dumb Things She Does
Dumb Things He Does

send $11.50 plus $3.95 shipping and handling to:

Books, Etc.
PO Box 1406
Mukilteo, WA 98275

or have your credit card ready and call:

(800) 917-BOOK

DUMB THINGS HE DOES . . .

7. Three pairs of shoes are more than enough.
8. You don't give a flip if someone doesn't notice your new haircut.
9. You can watch a game in silence for hours without your buddy thinking, *He must be mad at me.*
10. If you retain water, it's in a thermos.

If you are feeling brave, please continue reading this book by turning it over and turning to page 65 to begin reading *Dumb Things We Both Do.* Thanks for taking the time!

EPILOGUE

WHY IT'S GREAT TO BE A GUY

✳ ✳ ✳

OK men, you've done a great job in reading this much. If you are feeling a bit overwhelmed right now, let me leave you with a few thoughts (which were anonymously sent over my e-mail).

Why It's Great to Be a Guy

1. Bathroom lines are 80 percent shorter.
2. When clicking through the channels, you don't have to stop on every shot of someone crying.
3. You can be showered and ready in ten minutes.
4. Your underwear costs $7.50 for a pack of three.
5. None of your coworkers have the power to make you cry.
6. You can quietly enjoy a car ride from the passenger seat.

DUMB THINGS HE DOES . . .

are seduced. Should the women have said no? Absolutely! But your job is to keep the walls of your marriage secure; don't leave the door open for the enemy to get in. Find out what makes your wife feel loved, and then do it! Do what it takes to have a great marriage!

You can!

Make a small gesture today to romance your wife, and plan a bigger one for the future.

Stop Courting Your Wife

All in all, we had a great time and left (together) more in love than ever.

Now, I understand that this example is a pretty elaborate way to romance your wife. You don't have to come up with something so fancy. In reality, it's the little everyday things that build and strengthen a marriage. Although I will admit, a big event every few years can only help! What touched me about the whole New York event was that he did simple things that made it special. Because he knew my favorite movie was *Sleepless in Seattle* he planned our weekend accordingly. He could just as easily have said, "Holly, how about taking a trip to New York?" Then we would have taken an ordinary trip. What made it special was the surprise. (I love surprises!)

Your wife is the most important woman in your life; let her know it. I have had a few conversations with some men over the years who were having extramarital affairs. They were spending time, energy, and money, trying to conquer the new woman. If each of these men had taken that time and that energy and had spent it courting his wife, he would have the marriage he wanted. Don't look outside of your home for fulfillment.

I have also known women who weren't feeling loved (our number-one need) by their husbands, and so when some smooth-talking man, sent by the enemy appears, these women

43

Dumb Things He Does . . .

Of course, I immediately called my good friends and asked to borrow nice dresses. (Women do this!) Seven o'clock in the morning is not too early for good friends! I got my kids off to school with extra hugs to last the weekend. I was taken to the airport and given a note I was supposed to open on the plane. (I actually waited and did this!) This third note was the sweetest yet. In it, he told me how much he loved me and how much he was looking forward to some days alone with me. He told me he had some fun things planned and that we were going to have a great time. He also wrote that a limousine would be picking me up at the airport and taking me to the Empire State Building. On the plane, I proceeded to share my story with anyone around me who would listen, and by the end of the flight, there were more than a few people excited for me!

Once I arrived at New York's JFK airport, the driver met me and ushered me to the awaiting limousine. The music from the movie *Sleepless in Seattle* was playing in the limo. Philip had thought of everything! I was taken to the Empire State Building, and there I met the most wonderful husband in the world! We had four great days—in an exciting city. He had planned things I like to do: high tea in a fancy hotel, a show on Broadway, a carriage ride through Central Park. As well as some things he likes: a Yankee game and a visit to the David Letterman Show.

Stop Courting Your Wife

HIS

I read this note a few times and could hardly believe it! Philip, knowing my favorite movie is *Sleepless in Seattle* (a movie in which the couple meets on top of the Empire State Building), and knowing how much I love surprises, had certainly planned one for me. As soon as I stopped jumping up and down, I realized there was another envelope on my kitchen counter. I tore open that envelope and read note number-two:

Dear Holly,

What are you doing standing there? [Now how did he know that?] You have four hours to get ready. I have arranged someone to take you to the airport and someone to take care of the kids for the 4 days we are gone. We will have at least one fancy night so pack a nice dress! I have already left for New York so that I will be there to meet you at the top of the Empire State Building.

Love,
Philip

After I read that note, I was laughing and crying at the same time. I felt so loved. He had planned such a wonderful surprise!

Dumb Things He Does . . .

home and watch television, or work on your car, or work on the computer all night. You might find that we would be a tad unresponsive in the bed. If you want the reward of intimacy, you have to plant the seeds. You have to talk to us.

Romance is important to us, and rather than resent it, just accept it. The occasional gestures, such as a flower, phone call, date, gentle touch, or kind word, go a long way toward creating a happy home. (By *occasional,* I mean daily!) Try something—anything. Be creative. Find out what she likes.

A few years ago, coming home from church after a Wednesday-night service, Philip told me that he would be leaving for work early the following morning. When I woke up Thursday morning, he was indeed gone. I began preparing breakfast for our children and getting them ready for school when I noticed an envelope on the table with my name on it. I opened the envelope and read the note, which said:

Dear Holly,

If you love me, use the enclosed plane ticket and meet me at the top of the Empire State Building at 9:00 P.M. tonight. [Remember, we live in Los Angeles.]
I love you.

Philip

40

Stop Courting Your Wife

note, what touches my heart is that, at some point in his busy day, he took time to stop and think of me. Birthdays and anniversaries are obvious times for romance, but it is the out-of-the-way times that are really meaningful. I know that by bringing flowers or by leaving a note, he is saying, "I love you. You are important to me." Sometimes in the middle of the day, I'll get a quick phone call from him, to tell me he loves me. A soft touch, a gentle kiss, a squeeze of the hand as we are both busy about our day, really make me feel loved. Little actions like these open my heart.

Most of us have learned over the years that men tend to be visual creatures and women tend to be auditory. This means that you are stimulated or moved primarily by what you see, which is why you like us to shop at Victoria's Secret, and why we are touched by the words you say. Most high-school boys have figured this out, and unfortunately, some have used this to manipulate a young woman into having sex. They say, " I love you. That's why I want to sleep with you." And the young girl, moved by what she hears, not by his physique or lack of one, complies. You can bet, I will be teaching my daughter not to believe everything she hears, and that her virginity is priceless.

One of the reasons women talk is to create intimacy and a sense of closeness. Because intimacy for us is linked to what you say, it's important that you don't work all day, then come

DUMB THINGS HE DOES . . .

In the Book of Ephesians, chapter 5, God directs the husband to love his wife. This direction is given three times in the same chapter. God must realize how important it is for women to feel loved. In fact, feeling loved is our number-one need. We are not wrong because we need to feel loved. We are not wrong because we like to be romanced. You might resent our need for love and affection, but it doesn't change the reality that God made us with the desire to be cherished. I suggest that, rather than resenting this quality in us, you seek to fulfill the need to the best of your ability—because in a marriage, you are the only one who can!

While the number-one need of most women is to feel loved, your wife is probably different than I am in how she needs to have love demonstrated to her by her husband. I will make a few suggestions for you, but be sure to check with her to see what *she* needs. Many times after I have read a book on men or marriage, I ask my husband if the information presented applies to *him*. I don't want to learn how to be a good wife to the men "out there"—I want to be a good wife to *him*.

There are some fairly easy ways to court and romance your wife, and there will be some ways that take a little more work. I love it when Philip brings me flowers for no apparent reason or leaves a note for me to find. But more than the flowers or the

38

HIS

Chapter Four

Stop Courting Your Wife—
We Want Romance Till We Die!

AS WOMEN, WE HAVE GOTTEN HIP to the fact that you men are conquerors. Most of you feel that after you have put all the time and effort required to capture us (marry us), you can kick back and relax. Often a man's passion for romance dwindles a bit. The problem with this is that *our* desire for romance and *our* need to feel cherished doesn't disappear after the honeymoon! The husband who switches from overdrive romance before the wedding, to cruise control after marriage, is asking for trouble.

Not Growing Up

toward self-centeredness. Find a wise man to whom you can be accountable, and get going! Are you a man making the transition to being a father? Don't give up! Be encouraged. You can do this. You were created to do this. Your family, your church, and your world are counting on you to do your part. (No pressure there!)

> ## So, grow up already! Make the journey from boyhood, to manhood, to fatherhood.

DUMB THINGS HE DOES . . .

He had patience, even when surrounded by people who didn't have a clue what He was about. He loved, even when He knew He would be betrayed. He was a father. He could do this because His destiny was determined. You can too.

Your destiny, your purpose, has been decided. You were not created just to take up space on the planet, but God has a plan for your life. In the Book of Jeremiah, chapter 1, verse 5, God tells us,

> Before I formed you in the womb I knew you. Before you were born, I appointed you. . . .

Your birth was not an accident no matter what anyone has told you. As you discover the purpose for which you have been created, a new strength will rise within you. You will be able to give freely to others. Remember, your purpose will always include helping other people and will never be at the expense of your family.

I recently heard a song by Randy Travis that asked the question, "When a tough choice needs to be made, will you make it with the spirit of a boy or the wisdom of a man?"

Discover where you are in your journey. Are you still a boy? It's never to late to grow up. So get started. Drop the tendency

34

Not Growing Up

ever, the dream in your heart should never be at anyone else's expense. I have no problem with the idea of this man's wanting to be an actor, but when the work stopped coming in, it was his responsibility to find other work. As a man, your job is not only to take care of your needs, but those of your family, as well.

Perhaps there are many of you who did not have a strong, godly father to set an example for you. Don't let that be your excuse! There likely are men in your church who can mentor and support you. I also rejoice at the Promise Keeper organization's ability to draw thousands of men together. Make a plan to attend one of their meetings. Your family is depending on you.

The last transition a male can make is from being a man, to being a father. A father is someone who gives to others without expecting anything back. A father gives love when none is coming back. A father is more concerned about his wife's needs than his own. This is the man so secure in who he is, so secure that God will provide for his own needs, that he can freely give. A father is not just an older man, but a different person.

Being a father isn't dependent upon having children. Jesus was a great example of a father. He gave, He served, and He laid down His life without expecting anything in return. He inconvenienced Himself for others. He worked even when exhausted.

man is an entirely different person than a boy; he's not just a bigger boy. However, a lot of what we see in our city, as well as the church, are "boys in men's bodies."

Because Philip and I live in a city where the entertainment industry is prevalent, we come across a number of people involved in that industry. I worked as an actress for about fifteen years, and I love the creative, energetic, passionate aspect of that industry. It does, however, perpetuate the boyhood syndrome in some males. Some pursue their dreams at the expense of the real-life priorities. Whether you are pursuing your dream in the area of business, the entertainment industry or even ministry, providing for your family must be a priority.

I heard of an actor who was married and had children. At one point in his career, he was making good money, and then he had a few lean years. Rather than pursuing other work, his wife had to get a job to bring in finances. She began to be the sole breadwinner, supporting the family while he remained frustrated about having no work. Because he was looking for ways to make himself feel better, he began to spend money on extravagances they could not afford. As this continued, the marriage dissolved.

It is important to have a dream, a vision. If you don't, you will be frustrated, as well as frustrating those around you. How-

tion of the Jewish Bar Mitzvah, we don't honor this change. I believe we have a generation of males who are old enough to be men, and yet still act like boys—self-centered and self-indulgent, looking to have their own needs met. When those needs aren't met, they pout, throw tantrums, display uncontrollable anger, hit someone, and slam doors. This behavior is not acceptable in my child, and it is disgusting to see in a thirty-year-old male, and yet I have seen it. I have seen males who should be men, displaying all of the above-mentioned behaviors. And if that behavior doesn't accomplish the desired results, then they play all day, abandon responsibility, don't follow through, and aren't able to make a decision. Being a man means realizing the world does not revolve around you. Right now, Philip and I are planing the celebration of our son, Jordan's, transition, during which we will no longer see him as a child or treat him as a child. He will be given more responsibilities, and the training for manhood will begin.

Most of you probably did not have a ceremony or celebration that marked your journey into manhood. In fact, perhaps you were never made aware of the importance of "putting away childish things." But, it is never too late to grow up! A *boy* is concerned with taking care of himself, a *man* not only takes care of himself, but can do it while also taking care of others. A

that must change as we grow, if we are to live a victorious life. You can't be the eternal Peter Pan!

As you pursue your walk with God, you must make the journey of growing from a boy, to a man, to a father. There is nothing wrong with each stage, as long as you are committed to moving to the next stage.

A boy is a child. He is entirely focused on getting his needs met. This is not bad, this is what children do. My son, Jordan, is eleven. When he began his life as a baby, Philip and I had to meet all his needs. When he was hungry, we fed him. When his diaper was dirty, we changed it. When he hurt, we held him. We, as his parents, were responsible for seeing that his needs were met.

As he grew, he began to be able to meet his own needs. If he wanted something, he could get it. He wasn't concerned with helping other people get their needs met, but he could take care of his own basic needs and wants. This is not a bad stage to be in. There is nothing wrong with being a boy between the ages of four and thirteen. In fact, that is the only time a person should be a child.

Sometime in those early teen years, the boy should begin the transition to manhood. In many civilizations around the world, this transition is celebrated. In America, with the excep-

CHAPTER THREE

Not Growing Up—
OK, You Can Keep Your Nintendo

When I was a child, I spoke as a child, I understood as a child, I thought as a child; but when I became a man, I put away childish things
—1 Corinthians 13:11

THIS SCRIPTURE IS NOT TALKING about putting away your Nintendo 64, your surfboard, your roller blades, or your skis, so relax! It is talking about thoughts, words, and actions

Not Knowing Your Job

Being the spiritual leader means you set the example for how to love, how to forgive, and how to obey. Your family is watching! Your wife and your children pick up on what you do. If you yield to God and submit to authority, your family will yield to you and speak well of you. If you are committed to excellence, you will have a family of champions. *You* set the tone.

> **Understand your job as a husband, and even though it's a challenging one, go ahead—become great at it!**

These are just a few ways women are different than men. There are plenty of books out there, explaining in much more detail. Go get one and continue learning!

Your wife probably has a different personality makeup than you do. She probably has strengths where you have weaknesses and weaknesses where you have strengths. Is she outgoing or quiet? Is she organized or spontaneous? What are her strengths? What are her weaknesses, and how can you help her? (It's not by preaching at her or getting angry at her weaknesses!) As you learn to live with and understand your wife, you will make the journey from being angry about the differences, to understanding them, to tolerating them, to rejoicing in them. God made your wife just how she is, and He loves her just how she is. You need to also!

Be the Spiritual Leader of Your Home

This means you set the spiritual atmosphere for your family. Don't let your wife be the only one who prays for the children or is active in church. Philip is the one who has created a great spiritual balance in our home. He has made serving God fun, practical, and life changing. He teaches the children in real ways how to be thankful, kind, and respectful. He has bought family devotional books so that, as a family, we can learn together.

reasons why I shouldn't feel that way because this person hadn't been a good friend anyway. He said that she had been flaky and unfair to me, saying cruel things about me, and so wasn't it good we weren't friends anymore? Now, while all of this is true, did this help me deal with my hurt heart? No! What I needed was for him to hold me and let me talk about it. I needed him to say, "I'm sorry you're hurting. What happened was terrible." I needed an ear—someone to talk to—not a list of what I should feel and why. Nowadays when I'm hurt or stressed, Philip just holds me and listens and listens and listens! What a guy!

Women are different in so many ways. We talk a lot more than men do. (You've probably noticed this!) By the time you are home from work and winding down, we are just getting warmed up and have a lot more words to say! While your wife should be your friend, she is not your "buddy." She needs to be communicated to differently than you would to your male pals. One of the reasons we talk is to create intimacy. So when you talk to us, if you would, go a little beyond just the mere facts. You might actually have to string together more words than "What's the score?" or "What's for dinner?" We do want to know your feelings. One of the fruits of intimacy is a great sexual relationship, which I'm sure you're interested in! So please learn how to communicate your feelings. Ask questions of your wife about her day. Then listen, being patient when she's sharing.

because feeling loved is a woman's number-one need. Ask her what you can do that will help her feel loved. In the passage in Ephesians, loving your wife is mentioned three times. Maybe God thinks it takes more than once for it to register!

Live with Your Wife, Offering Understanding, Giving Honor, and Delighting in Her

Work on knowing your wife. What are her dreams, hopes, and fears? What excites her? What hurts her? What makes her cry? Know her.

Another way to know her, is to understand that, as a woman, she thinks quite differently than you do. God did design us to be different than you, because then, together, we are complete. Take the time to study the uniqueness God has placed in your wife. The more you understand her as a woman and as an individual, the less likely you are to be angry with her. Remember, we are not you. We will do most things quite differently, and that doesn't make us wrong.

When we are feeling stressed or hurt by a situation, usually we want your compassion, your understanding. We don't necessarily need you to fix it, so put the tool belt down! One time, my feelings were really hurt by a friend's betrayal. I was devastated. As I sat next to Philip on the couch, he began to give me

to be the head of the church because He laid His life down for it, not just because His Father owned the company.*

Philippians 2:5–7 says,

> Let this mind be in you which was also in Christ Jesus, who, being in the form of God, did not consider it robbery to be equal with God, but made Himself of no reputation, taking the form of a bondservant, and coming in the likeness of men.

You are not the head because you say it; you are the head by being it. Jesus didn't come to be served, but to serve. As the head, you will need to confidently take on the role of a steward.

Love Your Wife as Christ Loved the Church.

Christ loved the church so much that He gave his life for it. I don't think God is asking you to physically die for your wife. Sometimes that would be easier than what He is asking! He is asking you to die to your ego, your needs, your wants, and your reputation. This is what Jesus did for His church, even knowing that He would be betrayed. Loving her, means you are as concerned about her future as your own. Demonstrate your love,

---

* P. B. Wilson, *Liberated through Submission* (Eugene, OR: Harvest House, 1990) p. 73.

own husbands in everything. Husbands, love your wives, just as Christ also loved the church and gave Himself for her, that He might sanctify and cleanse her with the washing of water by the word, that He might present her to Himself a glorious church, not having spot or wrinkle or any such thing, but that she should be holy and without blemish. So husbands ought to love their own wives as their own bodies; he who loves his wife loves himself.

Husbands, likewise, dwell with them with understanding, giving honor to the wife, as to the weaker vessel, and as being heirs together of the grace of life, that your prayers may not be hindered.

Be the Head of the wife as Christ Is Head of the Church.

What does it mean to be the head? It means you are the final decision-maker. It means that even if you don't make more money than your wife does, you are responsible for the budget. Bunny Wilson, in her book *Liberated through Submission*, says it like this:

As the head you are sacrificially committed to every aspect of her growth. It means you are willing to take full responsibility for her protection and guidance, and leaving her the room to develop into the woman God designed. Christ got

HIS

Chapter Two

Not Knowing Your Job— You Do Have One

IT TAKES A MAN SURRENDERED to God's Word to carry out God's order. God has given men some very specific leadership assignments, which when accomplished, glorify His kingdom. Let's look at your four-part job description listed in Ephesians 5:22–28 and in 1 Peter 3:7:

Wives, submit to your own husbands, as to the Lord. For the husband is head of the wife, as also Christ is head of the church; and He is the Savior of the body. Therefore, just as the church is subject to Christ, so let the wives be to their

Not Leading Your Family

are leading. Keep growing and learning to be the best leader you can be.

> **Your family will follow the leader; make sure you're leading in the right direction.**

DUMB THINGS HE DOES . . .

first lesson, I learned one of the most important rules. Our teacher told us that Philip's job was to lead, and mine was to follow. Imagine that! Kind of like life. And even though Philip and I heard her give us the rule, it still took work to act it out. At some point in my growing up years, I had learned some dance steps, so I picked up very quickly the dances our teacher was demonstrating. Philip had never done any dancing, so he had a harder time. The temptation for me was to then lead because I knew what we were supposed to do, but our teacher soon stopped that! And she told Philip that in his leading of me, his movements and cues have to be definite not hesitant. If he hesitates, I won't know the right move to make, and we'll end up in a puddle on the floor!

Likewise, husbands, you need to be the leaders of the home. Ask God for wisdom in the decisions and actions you need to take, and then lead. Don't be hesitant or passive. We need you to lead. It's easier to follow a leader who is actually leading. You can do it!

Be confident of this very thing that He who has begun a good work in you will complete it . . . (Phil. 1:6)

God is not a quitter. Don't you be one either. If you don't like how your wife or your family is following, change how you

Not Leading Your Family

by bossing others around; it is not. Jesus didn't boss his disciples around. He led them by example. He wasn't trying to prove anything. Nowhere in the Gospels does Jesus say, "I'm in charge, so submit!" He was confident in who God created Him to be, so then He could give, be a servant, and not be afraid of losing His position.

God has called you to be the head, to be the leader. You don't need to prove it or fight for it. Just learn to live it. In the Book of John, chapter 13, we read the story of Jesus washing the feet of His disciples. In verse 3, Jesus washed their feet, knowing who He was. That's why He could serve, give, and perform such a humble task—because He knew who He was and that the Father had given all things into His hands. Serving in no way diminished Him.

The disciples were shocked that Jesus as the boss, the king, would humble himself and wash their feet, but what He was doing was showing them His leadership style. He is the head of the church, and yet He didn't demand or even ask that the disciples wash His feet. He washed theirs. He was showing them that to be the leader is to be the number-one steward. Lead your home by example, by serving, not by demanding.

Recently Philip and I started taking ballroom-dancing lessons. He took the initiative and signed us up for lessons. At the

way. It was difficult! I liked sitting on the throne of our home and being queen. God started talking to me about His order. He said that if I wanted my husband to fulfill his call, and if I wanted our family healthy, I would have to get off the throne. I then offered, "How about if I share the throne with Philip?" God was not impressed!—so I got off.

At the same time, Philip was learning about leading, taking responsibility, and being strong. He began leading by example. He did not lead by being domineering. As I saw Philip yield to God's order by submitting to God and to those in authority over him, then I began to submit. As he provided for our home. I began to take care of it. We women learn by example, so if your wife is not yielded to you, perhaps she doesn't see your example of submitting to God, your boss, your pastor, or others in authority over you.

There has been such an emphasis on submission among married women (and rightly so—I'll talk to them in the other section) that, basically, the responsibility of the man in submitting to God's order has been ignored. Leading your family won't always be an easy job, but it is one you have been called to do. And because you've been called to do it, God has placed within you all that it takes to be a man who can lead your family into the next millennium. Many men think the best way to lead is

Not Leading Your Family

has another family to abandon. As a man, if you are married, you need to be discovering who you are and what your strengths are from within the marriage. Strengths and weaknesses are revealed under pressure. Let the day-to-day work of your marriage reveal who you are.

Leading your family is an active position. Sadly, I have seen so many husbands destroy their families with their own passivity. They aren't watching who or what they let in their home. They are off pursuing some dream, and the wife has to bring in the finances and maintain the fort. And let me tell you, if a man gets off the throne of his home—the place where God has ordained him to be—the wife will usually sit on it (no matter how wrong it is). Remember, our challenge is to submit to the husband's leadership, though we'd rather have the position of headship, so if you are going to offer it to us, we'll take it. The end result of this is a very messed-up family. Healthy families come from doing things God's way.

I was raised, like a lot of women from my generation, with an attitude that anything a man can do, I can do better. Submission to a husband went out with the bra-burning ceremonies of the seventies. Well, needless to say, I was in for a bit of a shock after I got married. I did love God, and I wanted His best for our family, so I began to work really hard at doing it His

15

ground if he wanted to eat and provide for his family (Gen. 3:17–19). No longer was his life one of leisure! Now he was called to work and to lead a wife, who didn't really want to be led.

Part of the curse women deal with is that our desire is for our husband's position (Gen. 3:16). As women, we are called to yield to God by submitting to our husband and to his leadership, even while inside we are battling with wanting the control, with wanting his position. Because of this, I recognize that we are not always easy to lead, however that doesn't change God's call for us, or for you.

Likewise, men are called to submit to God and lead their families, when they would much rather play with the boys, or even with other women. There are plenty of men around the country and in the church who are in absolute rebellion against God's order, and so they are fleeing their responsibilities. I read an article about a famous actor who was quoted as saying that he was divorcing his wife and basically destroying his family, because this particular time in his life was going to be "his time." He wanted to discover "who he was." There are times when we all want to abandon what's right and do something just for ourselves. Only, the fruit of that self-centered action will be grief. This particular actor, on his journey to fulfill his needs, met another young lady and got her pregnant. Now he

CHAPTER ONE

NOT LEADING YOUR FAMILY—
WE ARE FOLLOWING THE LEADER: YOU!

THE JOB GOD HAS GIVEN YOU men is not an easy one. Before I really understood your job description, I thought you guys had it easy. Now I don't think that. I have compassion for you as you choose to submit to God's plan for your life. He *must* think you can do it, because he made you a man!

As we read Genesis, we see that before Adam and Eve sinned and had to leave the garden, Adam had plenty of leisure time. His toughest job was naming the animals! God provided his food and gave him all he needed, including a wife. After the fall, Adam, yielding to God's leadership, submitted to Him by working the

Dumb Things
He Does . . .

HIS

yours. This book is not the ultimate guide to wedded bliss; it does not present all the answers to every problem. This book is just a small piece of the puzzle. There are many books on marriage out there; read some. There are wonderful seminars and conferences available to help us married people; go to one. A great marriage doesn't happen just because you want it, but because you want it enough to learn and grow.

I split this book into three sections, "Dumb Things She Does," "Dumb Things We Both Do," and "Dumb Things He Does." Read whatever section applies to your situation, or read them all. And after reading, *talk.* Talk to your spouse about what you've read. Do you agree with this point or that point? Have you done this particular dumb thing? (Let your spouse answer as to whether you have done one of the dumb things or not!) Remember marriages are worked out over a lifetime, so relax. . . . Even you—no matter how many dumb things you've done—*can* strengthen your marriage!

Preface

"Remind me that God hates divorce and that murder is against the law!" was a plea I made to a good friend a few years ago. I laugh about that comment now, but back then I wasn't kidding. Not only did it seem that our marriage just wasn't fun anymore, but maintaining it was too much work. Perhaps there have been times when you, too, have felt like that. Perhaps you are feeling like that now! Well, take heart; you are not alone, and there are some answers!

In this book I will present some clear, simple suggestions that certainly helped my marriage and that I believe will help

Contents

Preface ix

DUMB THINGS HE DOES

CHAPTER ONE: Not Leading Your Family—
We Are Following the Leader: You! 13
CHAPTER TWO: Not Knowing Your Job—
You Do Have One 21
CHAPTER THREE: Not Growing Up—
OK, You Can Keep Your Nintendo 29
CHAPTER FOUR: Stop Courting Your Wife—
We Want Romance till We Die! 37

Epilogue: Why It's Great to Be a Guy 45

Dedication

This book is dedicated
to those of you reading this;
to those committed to building
a strong marriage in a society
that so desperately needs
to see you succeed.
You *can* do it!

© 1999 by Holly Wagner. All rights reserved

Printed in the United States of America

Packaged by WinePress Publishing, PO Box 1406, Mukilteo, WA 98275. The views expressed or implied in this work do not necessarily reflect those of WinePress Publishing. Ultimate design, content, and editorial accuracy of this work are the responsibilities of the author(s).

No part of this publication may be reproduced, stored in a retrieval system, or transmitted in any way by any means—electronic, mechanical, photocopy, recording, or otherwise—without the prior permission of the copyright holder except as provided by USA copyright law.

Unless otherwise noted all scriptures are taken from the New King James Version, Copyright © 1979, 1980, 1982 by Thomas Nelson, Inc., Publishers. Used by permission.

ISBN 1-57921-203-4
Library of Congress Catalog Card Number: 98-83200

dumb things he does

holly wagner

dumb things
he does